GUINEA PIGS

Other titles in the series

Keeping and Caring for Your Pet

Fish: Keeping and Caring for Your Pet
Library Edition ISBN 978-0-7660-4185-1
Paperback ISBN 978-1-4644-0301-9

Kittens: Keeping and Caring for Your Pet
Library Edition ISBN 978-0-7660-4186-8
Paperback ISBN 978-1-4644-0303-3

Puppies: Keeping and Caring for Your Pet
Library Edition ISBN 978-0-7660-4187-5
Paperback ISBN 978-1-4644-0305-7

Rabbits: Keeping and Caring for Your Pet
Library Edition ISBN 978-0-7660-4183-7
Paperback ISBN 978-1-4644-0297-5

GUINEA PIGS

Keeping and
Caring for
Your Pet

Angela Beck

 Enslow Publishers, Inc.
40 Industrial Road
Box 398
Berkeley Heights, NJ 07922
USA
http://www.enslow.com

Contents

1

2

3

Choosing and Bringing Home a Guinea Pig

Guinea Pigs in the Wild

A wild relative of the domestic guinea pig

It is early in the morning in the Andes of South America. A bird of prey circles over the vast grassy plains. Otherwise, all is still. But wait . . . if you were to listen more closely, you would hear a faint rustling and a gentle, happy gurgling sound. Now take a closer look. The tall grass is a labyrinth of crisscrossed tracks. What could be making all this noise? At last you spot the culprits: wild guinea pigs!

Guinea pigs always march in single file—a legacy of their wild ancestors.

Walking in Single File

Guinea pigs travel in single file, with the largest guinea pigs at the front and rear, and the young well protected in the middle. Making constant gurgling sounds enables them to stay in contact; they are not able to see much through the long grass. The guinea pig group, consisting of about twenty animals, is on the way to one of its feeding areas. Once they have arrived, they begin to eat enthusiastically; they love fresh grass and herbs but also chew happily on dry stalks and leaves. Buds, flowers, fruits, and seeds are particular delicacies for guinea pigs, but they also enjoy bark and twigs of young trees and shrubs. And while the group gorges on its breakfast, one of the guinea pigs always keeps a lookout for predators.

Imminent Danger

Out of nowhere comes a sudden movement, an unexpected noise. The "security guard" gives a loud, piercing whistle as a warning, and within seconds, the entire guinea pig clan seems to vanish off the face of the earth. Within their extensive underground network, guinea pigs have numerous holes to hide in at the first sign of a threat—making them invisible to hungry predators. This is a clever strategy for a small creature that cannot see very much in the long grass and is unable to defend itself. Guinea pigs must always be on guard.

Hiding Underground

After a short time, the guinea pigs will take their first cautious view from their hiding places. Gradually they reappear and chatter among themselves with plenty of cooing, whimpering, and grunting, perhaps discussing what just occurred. Then they all decide to get back in single file for protection. Their natural habitats tend to be abandoned burrows of other animals because guinea pigs are not very good at digging. Morning turns to midday, and the bright daylight brings plenty of dangerous predators, so the guinea pigs will spend most of their time either grazing or napping in close proximity to the safety of their burrows.

Twilight

When dusk falls, the colony marches single file once again and makes its way to a new feeding ground. Most enemies have disappeared by now, and the guinea pigs can be at peace in their new pastures.

Family Disputes

However, life is not always peaceful within a family of guinea pigs. The alpha male lives together with his females and his young. When the young males become sexually mature, the alpha male can no longer tolerate them. He begins to make attempts to get rid of them, as they will rarely go voluntarily. The more aggressive males will try to stand up to the alpha in order to remain within the colony. In this case, serious fights can break out, using sharp incisors, and the weaker animal has to retreat.

Guinea pigs are naturally skittish and love to hide in small spaces.

Guinea Pig Zoology

→ **Order:** Rodentia (rodents)
→ **Family:** Caviidae (guinea pig)
→ **Genus:** *Cavia*
→ **Species:** *porcellus*

Guinea pigs are also called cavies. The domestic guinea pig, *Cavia aperea f. porcellus,* originated from the wild guinea pig, *Cavia aperea tschudii,* found in Peru. Whether the domestic guinea pigs of today really belong to the rodent category is still disputed among zoologists.

How the Guinea Pigs Left Their Homes

Direct Ancestors of the Guinea Pig

The original home of the guinea pig, or rather its direct ancestors, is in South America. The original habitat of wild guinea pigs (*Cavia aparea tschudii*), from which our domestic guinea pigs are directly descended, is limited to a fairly small area in the Andes. The guinea pigs' closest relatives are the Brazilian cavy, the rock cavy, the common yellow-toothed cavy, and the southern mountain cavy.

The Patagonian Mara and Capybara

Among the more distant relatives are the maras, which actually bear more of a resemblance to hares than to guinea pigs. It is possible to observe these two species of animal in most zoos. The capybara is also related to the guinea pig, which is difficult to believe at first glance because the capybara is the largest rodent in the world; it measures more than four feet long and weighs about 110 pounds. Another distant relative is the porcupine, an animal whose body and tail is partially covered in large spines.

From Wild Animals to Pets

Guinea pigs and their relatives have populated the earth for approximately forty million years, but it was not until fairly recently that they were kept as pets. They have lived in close proximity

to people for about ten thousand years, when, at some point, it was discovered quite by chance that these animals made tasty snacks. People began to breed guinea pigs in order to enrich their diet. In about 1200, American Indians in Central Chile used them as sacrificial animals and also for meat. Today one can still see them being sold in South American markets as food.

The Journey to Strange Lands

More than four hundred years ago, guinea pigs made their way over to Europe. They were brought there by sailors—whether to enrich the European palate, as an exotic attraction, or a "toy" for children is not exactly known. But what is known is that zoologists became very interested in these newfound creatures. The Swiss scientist Konrad Gesner wrote in 1554 about "the Indian rabbit or pig." Also, a very accurate description of guinea pigs can be found in German zoologist Alfred Brehm's *Illustrated Life of Animals*, written in 1875. Guinea pigs did not arrive in the United States until the 1800s.

Cuddly Pets

The fate of the very first guinea pig brought to Europe from South America is not known. However, it is known that by 1670, guinea pigs were brought over by Dutch sailors for their children. Less than ten years later, they were specifically bred

A guinea pig with such light fur would have little chance of survival in the wild.

Loveable and cute—who can resist a guinea pig?

for the purpose of being sold as quite expensive pets. But it was soon discovered that guinea pigs bred very quickly, so the trade died down. They could now be acquired quite easily and inexpensively. People realized that guinea pigs were cheap and easy to care for, which soon turned them into one of the most popular household pets.

→ What's in a Name?

Why are guinea pigs called guinea pigs?

Sailors brought guinea pigs with them across the sea to Europe. These stocky creatures have the same rounded figure as pigs, and they also make a squealing noise similar to a pig. In English, they were soon known as the little pigs that could be bought for one gold coin (a guinea). The French call them *cochon d'Inde,* meaning "pig from India." Christopher Columbus landed in America, thinking it was India, so this could be where the confusion started.

Guinea pigs took the world by storm and captured the hearts of adults and children alike.

Guinea Pig Breeds

Different fur colors are the deliberate result of breeding. Here is an example of a beige, smooth-haired guinea pig.

You only have to take a look in a pet shop to see that guinea pigs come in all different kinds of coats: solid colored or spotted, long or short fur, smooth fur or fur with lots of funny swirls and twists. Many of these varieties are certainly accidental, but there are also prize-winning guinea pigs that have been bred specifically according to a predetermined standard, with a set of very specific characteristics.

What Is a Pedigree Guinea Pig?

Pedigree guinea pigs must meet a specific set of characteristics. The standard of the breed dictates the size, weight, type of build, and, the most important differentiation of all, the color and texture of the fur.

Meet Some of the Breeds

A correct description of all the different breeds of guinea pigs is almost a science in itself. Breeders differentiate between color varieties, markings, and fur textures. The layperson can most likely differentiate between fur colors, but there may be a subtle variance in the type of fur. A detailed list of standards has been set by guinea pig breeders. Here are some examples of the different breeds of guinea pigs.

Alpaca
Curly, long hair with bangs and two rosettes of fur on the hips. It is basically a curly-haired Peruvian.

Coronet
Smooth, long coat with a fur rosette (also called a crown, whirl, or crest) on the head.

Crested

Smooth, short-haired with a rosette on the head. An animal with a white rosette is known as the American crested. The fur on the English crested is the same color as the rosette.

Smooth-Haired

Short, smooth fur; varieties are solid-colored, bicolored (Dutch), tricolored, or multicolored.

Merino

Long wavy fur with a rosette on the forehead.

Peruvian

Long-haired with bangs and two rosettes on the hips.

Rex

Curly, springy short fur that is very thick and stands up on end.

Rosette

At least eight whirly tufts spaced out over the body. The fur is stiff and coarse. Also known as the Abyssinian guinea pig.

Satin

Smooth, short, very shiny fur. They should never be mated with one another!

Sheltie/Silkie

Very long, smooth fur. The fur on the head is very short (no bangs).

Teddy

Dense, fluffy coat that stands up. The fur is moderate in length.

Texel

Long, thick, curly fur with short fur around the head. A curly-haired Sheltie.

Rosette guinea pig

Tricolored crested guinea pig

Silver rex guinea pig

Red and white Peruvian guinea pig

Coronet guinea pig

Bicolored texel guinea pig

Teddy guinea pig

The Ideal Guinea Pig Community

Guinea pigs feel much happier when they are part of a group.

Guinea pigs are very social animals and are only truly happy when they are together with their own species. So for all you guinea pig fans out there, the golden rule is "two is company"! It is not fair to keep a single guinea pig by himself. Even the most loving human being cannot be a replacement for a guinea pig's best buddy—another guinea pig!

Who Gets Along With Whom?

Most females will coexist peacefully right from the start.

Taking such factors as space into consideration (see page 18), two or more guinea pigs of either gender will generally get along very well.

Females With Females

Getting two or more females is usually the best combination. Within a group of females, the hierarchy is sorted out very quickly, ensuring a peaceful coexistence.

A Question of Age

Getting two females of slightly different ages is highly recommended. In a family of guinea pigs, the little ones are trained at around the age of three to four weeks. If you take two very young females of equal age, they will not have been properly reared and therefore will not have learned the correct social behavior. At the age of five to seven months, intense conflict may occur. If one of the guinea pigs is slightly older, it can "train" the younger one.

Dispute Among Females

If there is a lot of serious conflict between two females, it can help to add a neutered male to the group. Within a group of guinea pigs, there is always a hierarchy, which is dominated by an alpha male. In this case, minor squabbles are normal until the rank order has been established.

Males With Males

Contrary to widespread belief, males will tolerate other males. However, they must either be neutered before they reach sexual maturity (it is possible to buy guinea pigs like this) or have lived together from a very early age. In this case, do not mix them with females in the same cage.

Males With Females

Of course, males will tolerate females very well, as nature dictates. The only problem here is the fact that they will inevitably breed, which you as a guinea pig owner do not necessarily want! The male should be neutered before reaching sexual maturity. Once the animal reaches a weight of about eleven ounces, or at approximately four weeks of age, it is ready to breed. One advantage of early neutering is that the male can then go straight back to living with the female and does not need to be kept apart from the female for five weeks after the operation, as is necessary for a sexually mature male.

Guinea Pigs Getting to Know Each Other

If you have chosen two animals that have never shared an enclosure together, either with breeders, at pet shops, or in animal shelters, the two guinea pigs will have to slowly get to know each other. Use these tricks to help ease the process:

Sprinkle both guinea pigs with unscented talcum powder to disguise the odor of each animal. Then place them back to back in a neutral space where they can run around and investigate one another. Simply let the animals do what comes naturally— guinea pigs know the best way to make friends with each other. Only step in if one begins to attack the other. With older guinea pigs, it may be necessary to put them in separate cages, but have the cages facing one another so that they can see, hear, and smell each other and get to know each other very slowly.

Keep an all-female or all-male community so there is no chance that your guinea pigs will multiply!

Guinea pigs get to know one another by extensively sniffing each other's behinds and faces.

Guinea Pigs and Rabbits   Tip

It has long been recommended—probably mostly out of fear of any unwanted offspring—to keep a guinea pig in a cage together with a pet rabbit. However, it is increasingly becoming common knowledge that this arrangement is unsuitable. The two species have different behaviors and do not really communicate very well. A guinea pig is a lot smaller than a rabbit and may be on the receiving end of repeated attacks from the rabbit, causing constant stress. This is not fair to either animal and definitely a bad idea!

How to Find a Healthy Guinea Pig

Test
Are You Ready?

Answer the following questions to the best of your knowledge:

- [ ] Do I have enough time to care for a guinea pig, and am I prepared to look after her every day for the rest of her life? (Guinea pigs can live for up to six to eight years.)

- [ ] Do I have enough space in my house for a large cage?

- [ ] Am I able to cover all the costs of owning a guinea pig—not only the regular cost of food and bedding but also any unexpected trips to the vet?

- [ ] Can I take care of my guinea pig on my own, or will I need help from my family?

- [ ] Are my family members free from allergies?

- [ ] Are there any friends or acquaintances who would be willing to look after my guinea pig when I go on vacation?

Did you answer all the questions with a resounding "yes"? Great! Then you really are ready for a guinea pig!

What Is Your Preference?

Do you want a colorful, spotty, shaggy ball of fur, or would you rather have a solid-colored guinea pig with smooth, shiny fur? This is a decision that is completely up to you. The most important thing is that your guinea pig is healthy—take your time and choose your pet carefully.

Finding a Guinea Pig

There are several places you can go to choose your guinea pig. Almost every pet shop sells guinea pigs, as do individual breeders. Or perhaps you have a neighbor or friend who has some unwanted babies that need a new home. Also, do not forget there are plenty of guinea pigs at animal shelters that need homes.

Identifying the Sex

Make sure those two females you buy from a pet shop really are both females! If not, you could very soon end up with more guinea pigs than you bargained for! Also check that any female you have purchased is not already pregnant. See page 49 for how to identify the sex of your guinea pig.

Not Too Young

A baby guinea pig should weigh at least eighteen ounces before he goes to a new home. Around the age of eight weeks, his digestive system is developed enough to tolerate most kinds of food, and

he will also have had the chance to develop his social skills. Guinea pigs weighing fewer than eighteen ounces are too young and are not ready to be taken.

Health Check

No matter where you get your guinea pig, you should do a health check before you take her home, using the checklist provided. It will help you tell the difference between a healthy guinea pig and one that may have health problems.

Think It Over

Guinea pigs are very cute, and you might find yourself tempted to buy one on a whim. This is never a good idea! Before you decide to get a guinea pig, you should think carefully about whether you actually have the time to care for your pet every day for about six to eight years. But you will soon see that spending time with your guinea pigs can be great fun, and it certainly will not feel like a chore!

Healthy Guinea Pigs . . .

→ should be in separate cages according to their sex.

→ have rounded but not overweight bodies. They should be compact and well-formed but not too thin.

→ are ready to be taken home once they reach a weight of eighteen ounces, about eight weeks of age.

→ should have large, clear, dark, shiny eyes that glisten slightly. The eyelids should not be crusty or swollen.

→ should not have any sores on their noses, lips, or ears.

→ should not pant or breathe heavily.

→ have firm, not bloated, stomachs.

→ have mouths without any defects and should not be drooling. The teeth should be even and in a vertical position, and they should already be slightly worn down, not overgrown.

→ should have clean bottoms, with no incrustations or diarrhea.

→ should have thick, shiny fur without any parasites. The skin should not show any signs of infection, boils, lesions, itching, or irritation.

→ should smell of fresh hay and clean straw.

→ should move quickly, easily, and freely without any signs of limping or lameness. The legs or paws should not be swollen or damaged in any way.

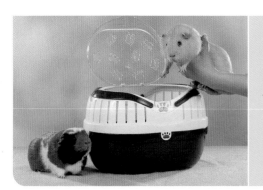

Moving Into a New Home

Take your new guinea pigs home in a pet carrier. It should be kept dark to calm the animals while they travel. Try to make sure that the journey is as quiet and smooth as possible. Do not allow the carrier to get too hot (for example, if it is in your car in the summer), nor should it get wet, cold, or exposed to any drafts.

Perfect Habitat

The Ideal Home for a Guinea Pig

It is a good idea to buy the guinea pig cage and the rest of the equipment a few days before your new guinea pigs arrive. This way, you will have enough time to get everything together, and you can devote all your time to your new guinea pigs on "moving day."

Size Matters

When you visit a pet shop, you will see many different kinds of rabbit and guinea pig cages, in all shapes and sizes. Make sure you choose the largest cage you can find. It does not matter whether it is really meant to be a rabbit cage. The American Society for the Prevention of Cruelty to Animals (ASPCA) recommends a minimum of four square feet of space for one guinea pig. Obviously, the more animals you want to keep, the bigger the cage should be. As well as the minimum cage size, you should also make sure the guinea pigs have somewhere to run around and stretch their legs for several hours a day.

Front Entrance

Guinea pigs are naturally peaceful animals that will take flight if something alarms them. They tend to be shy at the beginning, when everything is new, and can easily become panicked if something large and dark is looming over their cage from above. The genetic programming of the guinea pig will then tell him,

When it comes to a guinea pig's cage, the bigger the better! But remember that no cage can be a substitute for being able to run around in fresh air.

"Here's a predator—quick! Run!" even if it was just your hand about to reach down and stroke him. This is why you should always approach the cage from the front, reach in slowly, and pick him up—do not swoop in and pick him up from above because this will frighten him.

Two Compartments

Most guinea pig cages consist of two parts: a plastic base, which should be as deep as possible so the bedding and straw do not fall out and make a mess everywhere, and the wire cage that attaches to the base. This design is very practical when you are cleaning out the cage because you can place the wire cage over your guinea pig in the yard while you clean out the base.

Guinea Pig Duplex

A guinea pig duplex is a great idea. These are large and high enough for a second level, which the animals can access via a ramp, ensuring there is enough room for freedom of movement as well as a hideaway on one of the floors. This design is available from pet supply shops. If you are a crafty, do-it-yourself kind of person, you could build your own guinea pig home with help from an adult. A large selection of blueprints for guinea pig houses can be found on the Internet.

Wood Chips and Straw Pellets

Some pet shops sell coarse wood chips as small animal bedding. These are very good but have the slight disadvantage that they tend to scatter everywhere and make a mess. One way to overcome this is to add a layer of straw on top. Straw pellets are also suitable because although they are somewhat coarse, they soon soften when trampled underfoot and are absorbent and odor-binding.

Get everything ready for your guinea pig so you can have fun playing with her on her first day in her new home.

Bedding

The guinea pig's living area should always be kept clean and dry. The bedding should be absorbent and odor-binding. Use natural, biodegradable products without any chemical additives. The straw should not be dusty (this will cause skin irritations) or nonabsorbent because feces will remain stuck to the guinea pig's fur.

→ Unsuitable Bedding

Hay is not a suitable bedding because once soiled, the guinea pig will then eat it. The following are also harmful to his health: cat litter, newspaper, peat, sawdust, or very fine wood shavings.

Basic Necessities
Hideaways, Bowls, and More

Guinea pigs should have two food bowls: one for dry food and one for fresh food.

The new guinea pig cage is ready to be filled with fresh bedding, but what else can you add to make your new residents feel at home?

Hideaways
Guinea pigs live in burrows and tunnels and often feel a strong urge to retreat to the safety of a hideaway. A hideaway should be big enough for at least one guinea pig, preferably two. It might even be better to have two separate hideaways. There is a huge variety of hideaways available, but you should get one made of wood that is open enough to prevent a damp or humid atmosphere. A hideaway with a flat roof is best so the guinea pig can also use it as a lookout point. It also makes sense to have a hideaway with two entrances or exits so a lower-ranking guinea pig can easily leave the hideaway if he is pushed out by his bossy companion. Hideaways with windows are unsuitable because there is a risk the guinea pig could get stuck when he attempts to climb out the window.

A place where your guinea pig can hide is an absolute must.

Sturdy Food Bowls
Buy your guinea pig two food bowls, one for fresh food and one for dry food. The food bowls should be solid and heavy so the guinea pig cannot knock them over, and large enough so two guinea pigs can feed from them at the same time. Choose smooth bowls with no grooves or patterns so they are easy to clean.

Hayracks
Guinea pigs need a round-the-clock hay supply. The best way to keep the hay clean is to keep it in a rack. There are several models available. The rack can be hung on the cage or just kept loose, which is ideal for when your guinea pig is in the yard. The best designs are those with covers to prevent the guinea pig from climbing inside the hay.

Water
Make sure your guinea pig always has fresh, clean water available, either in a water bowl or a bottle attached to the cage.

Bottle or Bowl?
The water will stay cleaner and fresher in a bottle rather than a bowl. However, some guinea pigs may have difficulty drinking from a bottle because it requires more effort to get the water out, drip by drip. The bottle water will still need to be changed and purified on a daily basis; otherwise

algae will form in the bottle, which is harmful to the guinea pig. The water bowl should be positioned according to the guinea pig's natural head posture when he drinks.

Guinea Pig Furniture

Besides the necessary basic equipment, such as hideaways and hayracks, there are many types of guinea pig "furniture," which can spice up her living quarters: bridges, corks, tubes, shelters, ramps, and other things. Stick with the principle that "less is more" because all these items will take up space in the cage. You could buy several items but just use one at a time and change them around for variety. But when your guinea pig really needs change of environment, put her in a large playpen in the yard so she can let off some steam!

The Right Location

Where should you put the guinea pig cage? It should be in a place that has plenty of light but is not exposed to direct sunlight or drafts. A place where there is a lot of through traffic is unsuitable. Your guinea pig may get startled every time someone walks by. Look for a quiet place, but not somewhere that is hidden away in the corner, so the guinea pig can see everything going on in her new family. Guinea pigs like to have a good view of their surroundings and feel less threatened if they are somewhere up high, so you could put the cage on a table or a dresser. Just make sure it is stable and strong enough to hold the cage.

Above, below, and around: a variety of different objects will encourage your guinea pig to explore her surroundings.

→ Let Your Guinea Pig Decide

You will not know your guinea pig very well at first, so give her a choice of a water bowl and a bottle, and let her decide which one she prefers. If she chooses the water bowl, put it on a small brick or tile so it does not spill on the bedding, or you could keep it up on the second floor of her cage. The water bowl should also be stable and sturdy and cleaned on a daily basis.

The 7-Step Plan for a Tame Guinea Pig

The guinea pig will soon overcome his shyness and start to become curious about his new surroundings.

Your long-awaited guinea pig is finally here! Is he sitting huddled in a corner, looking terrified? Do not worry, this seven-step plan will help you get to know each other within a few days or weeks, depending on his individual nature. Then the fun can really begin!

Step 1:
Leave him in peace.

You may find this hard, but you will need to give him some peace! Place the open carrier into the fully equipped cage and wait. Sooner or later, the guinea pig will come out by himself.

a while to get used to all the new sounds around him before he stops being startled at the slightest noise and making a dash for his hideaway.

Step 3:
Make contact.

Once your guinea pig has become accustomed to his new environment, it is time for him to meet his new "herd members." Approach the cage at eye level and talk gently and quietly to him. The guinea pig will soon come up to the front of the cage to examine his visitors.

If your guinea pig hides, then let him be.

Step 4:
Offer a bribe.

The quickest way to get your guinea pig to feel comfortable with you is to offer him a delicious treat in your hand. He will be initially cautious but unable to resist coming to investigate and will soon lose his fear once he sees what you have to offer.

Step 2:
Watch him explore.

While your guinea pig is investigating his new surroundings, watch and wait from a distance. You will soon notice that he is incredibly curious, but it will take him

Step 5:
Stroke him.

Your guinea pig will already be curious about you as you approach his cage. Now it is time for the first physical contact. While your guinea pig is munching on the treat in your hand, talk to him in a soft and reassuring voice and use the other hand to gently stroke him.

Step 6:
Pick him up.

Once you have the guinea pig eating out of your hand, you could try to pick him up very carefully. Using slow movements, reach into the cage and place him in your arms. Hold him securely.

Step 7:
You did it!

Once your guinea pig learns to trust you, he will come running happily to the bars of his cage when he sees you, accept a snack from your hand, and be picked up without showing any signs of fear. Bravo! Mission accomplished. Now you can let him run around in the house as well as in a pen in the yard.

Once your guinea pig has been lured by a small bribe, he is ready to be stroked and picked up.

→ Respect His Privacy

Guinea pigs—just like us—do not like to be disturbed when eating, sleeping, or going to the bathroom! So even if the first introduction went well and your guinea pig has become well-adjusted to his new home, only play with him once he has finished these activities. Then he will be completely relaxed and ready for adventure.

Fresh Air
Outdoor Fun

The snow has melted, the first flowers have bloomed. The air is warmer, and the sun is shining. Everyone wants to be outside enjoying the beautiful weather, including your guinea pig! Let her play outside as much as possible, and as long as she is safe, she will take great pleasure in being outdoors. If the grass is dry and the temperature is around 64°F or above, you can take her outside!

On the Balcony

Unfortunately, balconies are not very suitable for guinea pigs; they are either too hot or too drafty, the flooring is not suitable (slippery tiles, cold concrete), and the railings of the balcony are rarely enough to stop guinea pigs from falling. But at the very least, you could put her out in her cage on the balcony. Please make sure she is not left in direct sunlight or drafts and that there is no dramatic temperature change between outdoors and indoors.

Making Your Balcony Guinea-Pig-Safe

With a little effort, you can make your balcony safe for guinea pigs. Cover all holes in the railing or screen with boards or dense wire mesh. Cover slippery, cold floors with straw mats (which will probably be eaten sooner or later!) or patchwork cotton rugs. Once you have done this, your guinea pig is free to roam the balcony but only under supervision, as cats or birds of prey will hunt guinea pigs that are left unprotected.

In the Yard

The easiest way to let your guinea pig enjoy the yard is to remove the top of her cage and place it over her on the grass. She will need to be provided with fresh water and hay.

Tip
Never Let Your Guinea Pig Roam Free in the Yard!

No matter how tame your guinea pig is, never let her run around the yard without first putting her in a cage or a pen. It would be very easy for her to escape, and you would probably never find her again.

If there is no shade, you can create some with an umbrella. Also, make sure there are no poisonous plants within reach. Now you can let the fun begin! But please keep an eye out for potential predators, such as cats or raccoons, which are perfectly capable of chewing through wire mesh, leaving your guinea pig cornered and defenseless.

A Treat for the Senses

Running around in the yard is a treat for your guinea pig's senses; she can enjoy the fresh air, smell new scents, and nibble on fresh grass and weeds. Feed her some fresh grass before you take her outside so that her digestive system has time to adapt to her new diet.

A Deluxe Playpen

Your guinea pig will enjoy being outside all the more if she has a larger enclosure, allowing her to really let off some steam. You can buy a large playpen from a pet shop, or you could build your own outdoor enclosure. There are many models and blueprints available on the Internet.

Threats From Above

An outside pen will also need a cover to protect your guinea pig from birds of prey, cats, and other predators. Just the pen by itself is not adequate protection because the guinea pig could be attacked or, at the very least, frightened by another animal that invades her enclosure. A cover with a wooden frame and sturdy, fine-meshed wire is ideal and needs to be a good fit for the enclosure to prevent cats and other animals from moving it.

What You Need for Your Guinea Pig's Outdoor Entertainment

→ a hideaway
→ fresh water and clean hay
→ a cover on the playpen for protection from predators
→ sufficient shade
→ shelter from the rain
→ no poisonous plants
→ no contact with wild animals
→ frequent checks on your guinea pig

Playing in the yard—this is when your guinea pig can really live it up!

Outdoor Entertainment

In principle, it is possible to bring your guinea pigs outdoors all year around, but it is not recommended. It is not enough just to put the cage outside in the yard. Outdoor entertainment must be supervised, and you may want to research more information on how to go about this safely. See the Further Reading section on page 72 for a list of books and Internet addresses.

What Your Guinea Pig Needs

Before You Buy

→ Before you decide to get a guinea pig, think twice about whether you can and want to be responsible for an animal for the next six to eight years.

→ Guinea pigs do not like living in solitude. So make sure you buy at least two guinea pigs.

→ When buying, remember that he is not old enough to go home with you until he is at least eight weeks old.

→ You can find guinea pigs in pet shops, from breeders, in animal shelters, through animal welfare organizations, and sometimes even from a friend or neighbor.

→ Be sure to buy all the basic equipment and set up the cage before you bring your guinea pig home.

Healthy Guinea Pigs . . .

→ have bright eyes and clean ears and noses.

→ have clean, thick, shiny coats that do not stick to their backsides.

→ move fast, without limping or lameness.

→ are compact, but not fat, and must not be too thin.

→ should only be bought if they have been kept in separate enclosures according to their sex.

Basic Equipment

For two guinea pigs, you will need:
- → a large cage, at least four square feet per guinea pig; the entry and exit should be at the front and not at the top
- → two food bowls
- → a water bowl or water bottle
- → a hayrack
- → bedding
- → a suitable location for the cage

Socialization

- → At first, simply observe your guinea pig and talk quietly and gently to her.
- → If your guinea pig does not seem anxious, then offer her a treat.
- → If she eats the treat from your hand without showing any signs of anxiety, then you can gently stroke her.
- → If she does not seem nervous, then carefully pick her up.
- → Only cuddle your guinea pig when she is not busy eating, sleeping, or going to the bathroom.

Out in the Fresh Air

- → You can buy an outdoor enclosure from most pet shops or perhaps build your own. For a short time outdoors, the wire cage cover is enough to get you started.
- → Make sure that the enclosure is escape-proof.
- → Do not forget to put a hideaway, water, and hay into the outdoor enclosure.
- → The enclosure should not be placed in direct sunlight or drafts.
- → Provide variety: different objects mean different adventures!
- → Do not forget to keep checking on your guinea pigs!

Feeding and Caring for Your Guinea Pig

Healthy Eating for Your Guinea Pig

What is your guinea pig's favorite pastime? Eating, of course!

A Varied Diet

Wild guinea pigs love any kind of fresh greens, as well as dried grasses, leaves, buds, bark, twigs, fruits, and seeds. These plants enhance a guinea pig's natural health defenses and promote well-being. The domestic guinea pigs' preferences are not any different, so make sure you keep your pet's diet as varied as possible!

A healthy, balanced diet with plenty of variety helps your guinea pig thrive.

Provide Plenty of Food

In order to stay fit and healthy, guinea pigs graze constantly and eat as much as they can. They have around forty to sixty tiny meals over the course of a day. Why? Guinea pigs have a very long colon, so their food is not moved along the colon quickly as in the case of humans. Their digestive system needs a steady food supply to keep the intestinal contents moving along the colon. In other words, every time food is digested, the food that is already in the colon moves a little farther along. This is why you need to make sure that your guinea pig has an around-the-clock food supply available—especially hay—so that he can eat whenever he needs to. If a guinea pig has been deprived of food for a sustained period and is then given a large amount of food, he will eat too quickly and too much at once rather than little and often, as his digestive system requires. The result is

Fresh greens and plenty of colorful vegetables mean that your guinea pig can eat until he is satisfied without becoming overweight.

that the contents of his intestine will not move along the colon. Instead, the food will rot in the gut, causing gas and very painful indigestion. This is why eating little and often is very important for a guinea pig.

Double Digestion

You may have already noticed that your guinea pig eats his own feces. Although you might think this is disgusting, do

not stop him from doing it because it is actually vital for his digestion. Guinea pigs do not just eat any feces; they carefully select the cecal pellets. These are formed by bacterial fermentation processes in the appendix and are actually partially digested food. It is from these cecal pellets that a guinea pig gets the majority of his nutrition, not from the first passage of food through the gut. This ensures he gets as many nutrients as possible from indigestible plant food, such as protein and vitamins (mainly vitamin B). This process also cleanses the inside of the colon.

Eating Is a Full-Time Job — Tip

For a guinea pig, eating is a full-time job. To avoid becoming overweight, he must eat the right food, particularly hay, fruit, and vegetables, as well as the occasional treat. Also, make sure he gets plenty of exercise out in the fresh air!

Chewing Helps Dental Hygiene

As with all rodents, a guinea pig's teeth never stop growing and need to be constantly worn down. The more a guinea pig chews, bites, and grinds his food, the better. It does not matter whether the food is hard or soft—the teeth are mainly worn down by being ground together.

Fresh hay should always be available for your guinea pig to nibble on.

→ A Guinea Pig's Basic Nutritional Needs

You can create a daily food plan for your guinea pig using these four basic components:

→ hay

→ water

→ fresh produce: herbs, weeds, fruits, and vegetables

→ a small amount of dry food

Daily Delights
Tasty Hay and Fresh Water

Hay–The Nuts and Bolts

Hay is the most important food for guinea pigs. It contains fiber (roughage), minerals, and trace elements; wears down the teeth when chewed; and can be eaten in large quantities without causing weight or gas problems. The quality of the hay depends on how many types of wild herbs are found within it as well as the mineral content of the soil in which it was grown, when it was mowed, and how it was dried and stored.

Hay and water are the mainstays of a guinea pig's diet, and he needs a constant supply of both.

What About Straw?

Straw is normally used as bedding rather than food. Nevertheless, guinea pigs do like to nibble on it. Straw is not as rich in nutrients as hay, but very high in fiber. Chewing on straw wears down the teeth

How to Spot Good Quality Hay:

→ It should contain visible herbs and many different types of grasses with leaves, flowers, and buds.

→ The stems should be eight to fourteen inches in length.

→ Good quality hay is green, not gray.

→ It should smell fragrant, not musty.

→ Hay should be grown in organic meadows and not polluted by pesticides.

→ Hay must be kept dry and dust- and mold-free.

and keeps a guinea pig busy. Because straw fields are much more frequently treated with pesticides and fertilizer than hay fields, they often contain more harmful residues than hay. So do not give your guinea pig too much straw, or you can buy straw that has been grown organically.

A guinea pig can eat hay around the clock without getting fat.

Water: The Elixir of Life

It may not appear that your guinea pig drinks very much water, but he will drink a fair amount, especially if he only has access to hay and dry food. Make sure he always has fresh water in his cage and when he is outside in his pen.

Clean Water

Whether your guinea pig uses a water bowl or bottle depends on his individual preferences. The most important thing is that the water is clean. The bowl or bottle should be washed out daily and then refilled with fresh water.

Dry Food

You can purchase a good quality dry food from any pet shop, which is available in many different forms and with added vitamins. However, if your guinea pig has a balanced diet, with lots of variety, he does not really need these because all the vitamins and minerals that he requires are in hay and fresh fruit and vegetables. If you still wish to buy dry food, pay attention to the ingredients. Some mixtures contain cereals, which a guinea pig's diet does not require.

→ Milk Is Bad for Guinea Pigs

Do not give your guinea pig milk. It is difficult for him to digest and contains lactose, which may lead to digestive disorders (diarrhea). Also be aware that distilled water is harmful to guinea pigs.

Cereal in Dry Food

Guinea pigs are not able to digest grains very well, and dry food does not sufficiently wear down their teeth. Grains fill him up too quickly and will make him overweight, much like the effects of chocolate on humans.

Plant Pellets

Look for dry-food mixes that contain plant matter and dried vegetables in the form of pellets. Pellets contain clover, alfalfa, coltsfoot, plantain, and nettles, among other things. He will get full more slowly and steadily without becoming overweight. A few pieces of carrot or beetroot make a nice accompaniment.

Only give your guinea pig a small amount of dry food every now and again.

Guinea pigs love parsley.

Hay, water, and a small amount of dry food are all very well and good, but there is still something missing from this diet: variety and freshness. Fruit, herbs, and vegetables are therefore an essential part of a guinea pig's daily diet.

Greens, Greens, and More Greens

Every food that is healthy and vital is green. Herbs and vegetables contain numerous vitamins and minerals, and a guinea pig requires about one ounce of greens per pound of body weight per day. The proportion of clover should not account for more than 10 percent of the total amount. Young nettles are especially valuable in the spring; they should be wilting or dried in order to reduce the risk of stinging.

Fresh fruit and vegetables provide numerous vitamins and minerals and are essential for the well-being of your guinea pig.

Gather Weeds and Herbs

Perfect for guinea pigs, weeds grow almost anywhere. It is best to pick them from uncultivated meadows or lawns and gardens, where there is an abundant growth of plants. Plants from lawns and gardens that have been treated, roads and roadsides, railway embankments, areas where people walk their dogs, and sprayed and fertilized fields are best left alone. Pick clean, dry plants and give your guinea pig as much as he can eat every day. Store the plants in an airy container and keep them somewhere cool.

Changing Your Guinea Pig's Food *Tip*

When you want to introduce a new item into your guinea pig's diet, do it gradually. Give him just a few pieces at first, and then increase the amount slowly, especially with fresh grass. It is high in protein and water and could cause indigestion if your pet is not used to it.

Fresh Is Best

Wherever possible, give your guinea pig freshly picked greens. The fresher they are, the better they will taste. Remove any uneaten greens from the cage after half a day, before they begin to wilt and rot.

Homegrown Greens

Homegrown greens from your windowsill will definitely be gratefully received by your guinea pig. You could grow these from seed mixes or grow fast-germinating plant species, such as grass, clover, and sow grain. Keep the soil moist and after about three weeks of growth, you can spoil your pet. If three weeks is too long to wait, you can buy cat grass from a pet shop instead.

Get Crunching: Delicious Vegetables

Guinea pigs love fresh, crunchy vegetables. Wash and peel them before you give them to your pet. You could surprise her by hiding them all over her cage or poke them through the roof bars so she has to reach up to nibble at them. This will encourage even the laziest guinea pig to move around and reach for her food. Any remains should be cleared away after half a day or so.

→ Fresh and Crunchy

Here is a list of a guinea pig's favorite greens:

- beetroot
- blue alfalfa
- borage
- broccoli
- carrot
- chamomile
- chicory
- coltsfoot
- cucumber (peeled)
- dandelion
- dill
- fennel
- Jerusalem artichoke
- kale
- lovage
- meadow yarrow
- mugwort
- parsley
- pepper
- peppermint
- plantain
- sage
- stinging nettle

If you are not sure what the plant is, it is better just to leave it. There is a risk that it could be toxic to your guinea pig.

Healthy Sweets
Fruit for a Fit Guinea Pig

Vitamin C

Because, like humans, guinea pigs cannot make vitamin C in their bodies, they must get it from their daily diet. Black currants, parsley, spinach, kale, green peppers, kiwi, broccoli, strawberries, and oranges are particularly rich in vitamin C. Guinea pigs require a variety of fruits and vegetables as part of a balanced, varied diet. This way, they will not require any additional vitamin supplements. Vitamin C is essential to health, but too much vitamin C can be harmful. For example, if your guinea pig suffers from arthritis, high doses of vitamin C can make it worse.

Fruit is another essential part of a guinea pig's daily diet. It adds variety and provides valuable vitamins, especially the all-important vitamin C.

Colorful Food Bowl

"A feast for the eyes" goes the saying, and if you give your pet a colorful variety of food in his bowl, you will notice his enthusiasm as he pounces happily on these tasty tidbits. Wash and peel the fruit if possible, and the same goes for vegetables. Make sure you give your pet plenty of fresh produce rather than just the odd apple core or two.

No Fussy Eater

There are not many fruits that guinea pigs do not like, but bananas are not recommended because they are very messy and full of sugar. Most guinea pigs are not too thrilled about very acidic fruits either.

Fruit Favorites

A guinea pig's favorite fruits are apples, pears, melons, grapes (not too many because they contain a lot of sugar), kiwi, strawberries, oranges, and tangerines.

Good to Gnaw

Fresh twigs and young shoots are extremely popular with guinea pigs. You can kill two birds with one stone because this type of food is useful and valuable: bark, buds, and young wood contain fiber, tannins, and oils. Nibbling and chewing such foods help a guinea pig wear down her teeth. Suitable cuttings to feed your guinea pig are from apple and pear trees, hazel, beech, poplar, linden, alder, and willow—as long as they have not been treated or sprayed. You could ask your neighbors for a few twigs if you do not have any of these trees in your own yard. They will probably be happy to get rid of a few trimmings.

Gnawing on wood keeps your guinea pig's teeth healthy and wears them down enough.

Fitness Food

To keep your guinea pig fit, do not just put fresh fruit and vegetables in her bowl. Hang some from the roof of her cage, push slices of apples into the bars, or hide pieces of vegetables all over the cage. This means she will have to hunt out her food and keep fit in the process.

Proper Nutrition for Guinea Pigs

→ Guinea pigs require fresh hay and clean water around the clock.

→ Make your pet's diet as varied as possible.

→ If you introduce a new food, only give her a small amount at first, and then slowly increase it.

→ The required amount of food depends on age, temperament, movement, cage size, the amount of exercise she does, and the ambient temperature.

→ Fresh produce should be washed and peeled. Remove any leftovers after half a day. Place fresh treats in the hayrack to stop them from getting soiled.

→ Provide a maximum of one tablespoon of dry food per animal, per day, spread over two meals.

→ Refrigerated food is not ideal for guinea pigs. Try to remember to take the food from the refrigerator a few hours before you feed it to her.

→ The following are not suitable foods for a guinea pig: cauliflower, cabbage or lettuce (which is often overfertilized and treated), stale bread, sweets, and cake.

FUN TIPS

Snack Ideas for Guinea Pigs

Tasty Tidbits and Cute Decorations!

For obvious reasons, tasty treats for your pet do not include chocolate candies or potato chips, but you will soon see how much he enjoys healthy snacks, and you can also eat them at the same time!

Hanging Bells

Hanging bells are easy to make and also look great! All you need is a few small ceramic pots, fresh vegetables, and string. Tie string around some vegetable pieces, then thread the other end of the string through the small hole in the ceramic pot. Tie this end to the wire at the top of the cage. Presto! You have your edible decorations!

Vegetables on the Rocks

For this fun food, you will need a brick. Now chop up different colored vegetables, such as carrots, fennel, and bell peppers, into small pieces and stick them in the holes in the brick. Your guinea pig will have to work to pull the treats out from the holes.

Stuffed Cucumber

Cut off a two-inch-long piece of cucumber. Dig out the inside with a spoon (you might need a responsible adult to help you). Fill the hole with some parsley, bits of red pepper, or any other vegetable your guinea pig likes. Then it is just a question of which to eat first: the filling or the cucumber?

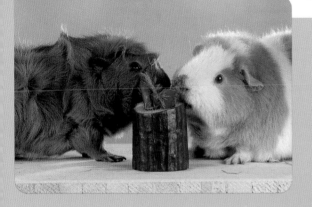

Fruit Kebab

Find some long, thick pieces of straw. Then push slices of soft fruit, such as kiwi, melon, or strawberry, onto the piece of straw to make a fruit kebab!

Funny Fennel-Men

You will need a fennel bulb, a small carrot, and some grapes. The delicate fennel leaves can be the hairstyle. Now carefully make a hole in the middle of the bulb with a kitchen knife and fit the carrot into the hole to form a nose. Then cut two holes above the carrot on either side and fit a grape into each hole to make the eyes. Your funny fennel-man is now ready to be eaten!

Grooming Your Guinea Pig

In addition to constant grazing, maintaining a beauty regime is one of the guinea pig's favorite pastimes.

Grooming for Short-Haired Breeds

Short-haired guinea pigs do not really need to be brushed or combed. But some guinea pigs may enjoy being stroked with a grooming mitt. They also enjoy having their back scratched in all those hard-to-reach places. At the same time, you can have a good look at his coat and skin to keep an eye out for parasites or irritation.

Grooming for Long-Haired Breeds

Long-haired guinea pigs need to be brushed regularly. If you perform this brushing ritual gently and lovingly, your guinea pigs will soon get used to it. Make sure you keep his fur trimmed so that it is off the floor; otherwise the long fur will drag on the ground and become matted and covered in urine. If you notice your guinea pig seems to be suffering from the heat in the summertime, give him a good haircut. The fur will grow back, and in the meantime, it will keep your pet cool.

Regular combing or brushing is only really necessary for long-haired guinea pigs.

→ Bubble Baths Are Banned

You should not attempt to bathe your guinea pig. It is usually not necessary. If he is dirty—for example, he has feces stuck on his fur if he has had diarrhea—clean the affected area with warm water and rub dry with a towel. Please do not use soap or shampoo.

From Beginning to End

While you are cuddling or stroking your guinea pig, take this opportunity to have a good look at him. Are his eyes clear and bright? Are his nose and ears clean? If the eyes are gooey or the ears are dirty, gently clean them with a soft damp cloth.

Also check the backside: the rear and the skin folds surrounding the genitals should be clean without anything stuck on them. On a male, the testicles and the area between the genitals and the anus should be regularly checked and cleaned with a damp cloth. Feel the abdomen and legs: Is the belly soft? Can the legs be moved around without pain? The better you get to know your guinea pig, the more likely you are to notice any changes, so you can quickly nip any problems in the bud.

Show Me Your Feet

Look at the claws on a regular basis. Often they do not wear down quickly enough and, in the worst case, will grow so long they will curl, which prevents the guinea pig from being able to walk or run. The soles of the feet should always be clean and without any cuts.

between them and where you make the cut. Clip in a horizontal direction across the claw. If the claws are very dark, you will not be able to see where the veins begin as easily, so only cut a tiny amount off each tip, though you will need to do this more often. Accidentally cutting into the quick will cause your pet pain and make him bleed. Get your vet to show you how to cut the claws the first time.

The claws should not be too long, and each tooth should be worn down evenly.

Trimming the Claws

Use nail clippers to trim long claws. This procedure is easier with two people, one to hold the guinea pig and the other to cut the claws. Use a good source of light so that you can see the red veins in the claws, called the quick, which contain nerve endings. Leave a good space

Say "Ahh!"

If the teeth get too long, this will affect the guinea pig's ability to eat. The vet will be able to tell you whether his diet is to blame or whether he has any birth defects, such as malocclusion (misaligned teeth). The right diet should help wear down the teeth in most cases.

Next, Please!
A Trip to the Vet

A guinea pig that spends a lot of time hidden away by herself may be sick.

A sufficiently large cage, lots of space to run around, loving care, plenty of hay, clean water, and a variety of fruits and vegetables are key to keeping your guinea pig healthy. You do everything you can to prevent your guinea pig from becoming sick or hurt. However, some things cannot be helped. If you suspect one of your animals is ill, take her to the vet as soon as possible.

Better Safe Than Sorry

It may take several trips to the vet to get an accurate diagnosis of the problem, so it is better to go at the first sign of a problem than not at all. Your guinea pig may have an acute and contagious infection, and the sooner she is treated, the better her chances of recovery.

Questions the Vet May Ask

The more precisely you can answer the veterinarian's questions, the better. Take your weight log and a feces sample if you suspect that your guinea pig has eaten something poisonous. The vet will most likely ask the following questions:

→ How old is your guinea pig?
→ How long have you had her?
→ Where is she kept, and how do you care for her?
→ Does she have an appetite/is she thirsty?
→ What has she eaten or drunk?
→ When did you first notice the symptoms?

This is how a healthy guinea pig should look.

If you notice any of the following symptoms, take your guinea pig to the vet!

- → abscesses
- → anal discharge
- → attempts to bite or squealing when touched
- → bald patches on the coat
- → blood in urine
- → bloodstains
- → cloudy or red eyes
- → consistently hiding away
- → constipation accompanied by foul-smelling feces
- → cramps
- → dandruff
- → delayed reactions
- → diarrhea, sometimes with blood

- → distended abdomen (the abdomen feels tight)
- → drastic weight loss
- → emaciation despite food intake
- → excessive fluid intake
- → excessive salivation
- → fecal changes–color or smell
- → feces sticking to the backside
- → frequent cough
- → frequent scratching (suspected parasites)
- → frequent sneezing
- → frequent urination
- → head shaking
- → ingrown, corkscrew-like, twisted claws
- → itchy ears
- → limbs at odd angles
- → long-lasting tremor
- → loss of appetite
- → loss of balance
- → loss of fur (not shedding)
- → lumps or bumps on the ears

- → matted fur
- → motionless for long periods
- → nasal discharge
- → nosebleeds
- → paralysis
- → redness, scabby skin
- → restlessness, lack of appetite, or thirst
- → shortness of breath
- → sores and scabs
- → swelling and changes to the mammary glands and/or sex organs
- → swelling of the lips
- → swollen eyelids
- → swollen or wounded soles of feet or legs
- → teeth long, curved, twisted, or with sharp edges
- → unnatural standing position
- → unusual head tilt
- → watery eyes

- → Have there been any changes in your pet?
- → Have the feces changed color or smell?
- → Is she making any unusual noises?

Treatment After Diagnosis

Once the vet has made a diagnosis, he or she will explain what to do. The vet will tell you whether your pet has to be kept separate from other guinea pigs. It is important to read any drug instructions very carefully and store the medicine in the correct manner. Check the expiration date as well. Do not stop or start a treatment without consulting your vet, and never give your guinea pig any drugs from your own medicine cabinet. Also, make sure you and anyone else who touches a sick animal washes his or her hands thoroughly afterward every time.

Keeping Your Guinea Pig Healthy

Delicious, crunchy greens and plenty of movement help prevent constipation.

If one of your guinea pigs is sick, she will require a lot of loving care until she is better. So that she regains her health as quickly as possible, make sure you follow the vet's instructions to the letter. If your guinea pig just has a small ailment, you could wait and see whether this clears up on its own, but if she is not showing any signs of recovery after a couple of days, then it is best to take her to the vet.

Hay and Blueberries for Diarrhea

If your guinea pig is suffering from a mild case of diarrhea, then keep her off the vegetables for a while. Just feed her some hay, a small amount of dried food, and fresh water. Some dried blueberries and a couple of willow twigs will also help. If there is no improvement after a couple of days, or she is suffering from severe diarrhea, then take her to the vet.

After a day or so of eating hay, any diarrhea problems should be resolved.

Juicy Fruits and Vegetables for Constipation

Mild constipation can often be fixed by a slight change in diet. Cut back on dry food for your guinea pig and instead give her foods containing plenty of water, such as fresh vegetables and fruit, as well as herbs and hay. Encourage her to move around more, and digestion should return to normal quite quickly. If her condition has not improved after two days, then take her to the vet.

Heatstroke

Guinea pigs cannot tolerate high temperatures because they do not sweat. If your guinea pig suddenly starts panting, trembling, becoming very excitable, or lying down, she may have heatstroke. Quickly move her to a cool place in the shade and cover her with a damp cloth or sprinkle her with some water.

If you have brought a new guinea pig home, it is best not to introduce her to your existing guinea pigs straightaway. Keep her separate from the others for around two to three weeks and keep a close eye on her to ensure there is no sign of disease. By doing this, you are protecting your already existing group from any unpleasant surprises (contagious infections, parasites, etc.).

Warmth

Sick animals need to be kept warm. There are several options for providing your guinea pig with extra warmth to relieve pain and loosen up tight muscles: pet with a thermometer—it should not be any higher than 73°F. When the treatment has finished, do not turn off the lamp straightaway. Instead, gradually move it farther and farther away from the cage.

Guinea pigs that are sick will seek out warmth. You could try placing him on a warm (but not hot!) cherry stone pillow.

heat lamps, microwavable cherry stone pillows or pet-safe heat pads, a simple box filled with hay, and blankets or fleece hideaways. If you use a heat lamp, place it a sufficient distance away from your guinea pig's cage. Check the temperature

Scents to Prevent Parasites

To prevent parasites, hang a fragrant bouquet of dry lavender, mint, tansy, wormwood, garden rue, and rosemary from your guinea pig's cage. Fleas and other parasites do not like these scents.

Vacations
Guinea Pigs and Travel

A guinea pig requires familiar situations, rituals, and routines. Anything new will unsettle her. In contrast, we humans tend to seek out a bit of variety in our lives and love to take vacations to new destinations. So how can these two very different needs be met?

Homebody

If you want to travel, then you will need to find someone you trust to look after your guinea pig. The best person would be someone who has guinea pigs and knows how to care for them. Ideally, your guinea pig sitter should visit your pets on a daily basis so they can remain in their familiar surroundings.

Stay With a Friend

The other option is to take your guinea pig and everything she needs to a friend's house. Make sure you show your friend in advance what your guinea pig likes to eat and leave your friend the phone number of your vet before you go.

Guinea Pig Boardinghouse

If you really cannot find anyone to help you look after your guinea pig while you go on vacation, you could try to find a boardinghouse for guinea pigs. Guinea pig charities, animal shelters, or pet shops will be able to advise you on somewhere she can stay.

Guinea pigs do not really travel well— they prefer to stay at home!

Traveling Guinea Pig

If traveling with your guinea pig is unavoidable, and as long as guinea pigs are allowed at your destination, then you will have to take her with you on your journey. To transport her, you will need a pet carrier with large airholes. While traveling, make sure she is not too hot or cold, and make sure there is enough hay and water available. Once you have reached your destination, set your guinea pig up in her own cage with all her familiar items around her.

When Guinea Pigs Get Old

Of course, every guinea pig gets old eventually. Some show noticeable signs of aging by the time they are five or six years old, but others may not slow down until they are around seven years of age.

Signs of Aging

Older guinea pigs have less need to exercise, and they do not like climbing over obstacles or onto elevated vantage points. To make life easier for your elderly guinea pig, provide her with a small ramp so she can get in and out of her cage more easily and also lower her food and water containers to make sure she can reach them. Although she may not show much interest in exercise anymore, she still needs to move around a bit. You could try playing with her and giving her lots of cuddles. If she is having a hard time chewing her food, then talk to your vet about giving your pet pureed food or soft food that is rich in vitamins. You could also give her very finely cut hay.

Food rich in vitamins is especially important for older guinea pigs.

Senior Living Quarters   **Tip**

Even old guinea pigs need their own kind around them. Often, the company of a younger guinea pig will give your senior pet a renewed sense of vigor. Guinea pig organizations can advise you on what is best for your senior pig at this stage of life.

Farewell

Elderly guinea pigs usually die in their sleep without any noticeable suffering. This is just a natural part of life. Take comfort in the fact that you gave your guinea pig the best life you could give her.

Two, Three, Four, or More
Guinea Pig Breeding

In a purely male or female living arrangement, you will not have to deal with any unwanted extras!

Breeding guinea pigs is best left to experienced breeders.

Guinea pig babies are very cute! Nevertheless, you should not be tempted to just leave your guinea pigs to their own natural devices. Guinea pigs are very prolific breeders and before you know it, you could have a huge family of them. So either get your male guinea pig neutered or keep an all-female or all-male group of guinea pigs.

Early Developers

Guinea pigs reach sexual maturity very early. Around the age of four weeks or from a weight of eleven ounces, males are able to reproduce, and a female guinea pig can easily get pregnant by this age. Therefore, it is very important to neuter the male early. Otherwise, your group of guinea pigs may get out of hand.

Separate Bedrooms

The last thing you want is to end up with a whole bunch of unwanted baby guinea pigs that you do not have time to care for. When you buy your guinea pigs, you must make sure that the males and females have been kept separate. Otherwise, you could be taking home a female that is already pregnant.

How It All Begins . . .

And if you are not careful to separate your guinea pigs, what happens then? A male will advertise his virility to a group of female guinea pigs. He will circle them, encouraging them to make physical contact and strut around, trying to find himself a mate. If he is successful, then within sixty-five to seventy-two days, the babies will be born.

Guinea Pig Babies Develop Quickly

Guinea pigs are precocial animals; they are born with their eyes open, a full coat of fur, and their incisor teeth fully developed. A baby can smell, hear, and respond to his mother, and when baby guinea pigs feel abandoned, they will complain loudly.

Milk and More

For the first three to four weeks, a guinea pig feeds on his mother's milk. The mother guinea pig only has two teats, which the little ones have to share, but they do not fight over the source of milk. Instead, they wait patiently for their turn. They also nibble away at any food the mother provides as early as the second day of life. The food supply for a small family of guinea pigs should be as varied as possible so the babies become familiar with lots of different types of food right from the start.

Learning for Life

During the first weeks of life, guinea pigs very quickly learn all they need to know. They begin to practice their social skills and communication within the

→ A Slight Difference

The sexing of guinea pigs, especially in young animals, is not an easy task. There is only a slight difference in genitalia—the female genitals are a "Y" shape, and the male genitals are an "I" shape (see picture). In some males, the penis may be inverted but not always. If you are unsure, get a vet or someone experienced to give you some advice.

group. In addition to getting to know their own kind, they also become familiar with the strange sounds and smells of their humans and should have as much human contact as possible. The more contact they have during the growth phase, the quicker they will become tame.

Out Into the World

By the age of six to eight weeks, a guinea pig should weigh about one pound and is now ready to go to a new home.

Responsible Breeding

Breeding guinea pigs should really be left to experienced breeders and not simply be done as an experiment out of curiosity. Breeders will know which pair of guinea pigs breed well together and how to care for pregnant females and newborn guinea pigs. A guinea pig breeder will be able to provide the right environment for the babies and also know how to find them loving homes when they are ready to leave.

At a Glance

My Care Plan

Your Guinea Pig's Daily Diet

Using these guidelines, you can put together a diversified daily menu for your guinea pig:

→ **Greens and Herbs**
a big bunch of dandelions, chamomile, yarrow, kale, and carrot greens

→ **Crisp Vegetables**
a carrot or 1/4 of a fennel bulb or 2–3 broccoli stems or 1/4 of a pepper or a 2-inch-long piece of peeled cucumber

→ **Juicy Fruit**
1/4 of an apple, 5 grapes, 1/4 of a pear, or 2–3 strawberries

→ **Dry Food**
one tablespoon of a mixture containing plant pellets without grains

→ **Hay and Water**
Always make sure your guinea pig has plenty of these.

Daily Care

Food

Mornings and Evenings
Remove any damp hay and uneaten food, and clean out the food bowls with hot water. Put half the daily food ration in the cage and fill up the hayrack.

Water

Change the drinking water at least once a day. Rinse out the water bottle or bowl with hot water and then refill with fresh cold water.

Exercise

Make sure your guinea pig has at least two to three hours out of his cage to run around. Let him play in an open area in the house or in his pen in the yard. Be sure to keep an eye on him. Take time to cuddle and stroke him as well.

Health Check

Are his eyes clear? Are his ears clean? Is his coat shiny? Is his belly soft? Is he exhibiting normal behavior? While you cuddle and play with him, give him a quick health check at the same time.

Weekly Care

Clean Out the Cage

Once a week, clear out the cage, wash it with hot water, and fill it with fresh bedding. Do not use any strong detergents to clean out the cage. Clean, hot water is enough.

Health Care

Give your pet a thorough health check once a week. Examine his fur, skin, eyes, nose, ears, teeth, paws, claws, and backside. Carefully examine his genital area, too.
Long-haired guinea pigs will need to be combed or brushed and, if necessary, trim a little off the fur so it does not drag on the floor.

Monthly Care

Cleaning

Check all equipment and cage furnishings. Any objects that have been gnawed or damaged or made dirty should be replaced.

Activities

Provide variety. Look for new accessories that will encourage movement and interest—for example, tunnels or tree branches. Add a few surprise treats, such as a food garland, for instance.

Understanding and Playing With Your Guinea Pig

Guinea Pig Behavior

Sight, hearing, smell—guinea pigs use all their senses to discover the world around them.

The more you know about your guinea pig, the better you will understand him, and the more fun you can have together. So keep your eyes and ears open—what can you learn about your guinea pigs?

Flight Not Fight

Guinea pigs are small and neither strong nor brave. So what do they do when they sense danger? They run as fast as their little legs will carry them and seek refuge in their hideaways. Guinea pigs are prey animals, and whenever they feel threatened, they immediately go into hiding. Not only do they feel threatened by their natural enemies, but also, when kept as pets, they are easily frightened by loud noises, new smells, sudden movements, or a large hand swooping down on them from above, like an eagle.

Approach at Eye Level

Guinea pigs are especially fearful of sudden movements above them, as it is their natural instinct to be wary of birds of prey in the wild. So it is best if you approach your guinea pig at eye level.

If a guinea pig feels threatened, he will make a quick dash to his hideaway.

Play with him and cuddle him while sitting on the floor, and put his cage on a surface at eye level. When you first bring your guinea pig home, everything will be new to him—new cage, strange sounds and smells, different humans, and perhaps other pets. As long as you are gentle with him, he will soon learn to trust you.

Shortsighted With a Panoramic View

Guinea pigs cannot see into the distance very well because they are rather shortsighted. However, they can see movements close by and have a good view of everything going on around them. In fact, they have an almost 360-degree view of their surroundings because their eyes are located at the sides of their heads, instead of at the front like in humans and other predators.

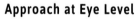

This means they do not have to turn their heads in order to see. However, because they are shortsighted, they can only see movement close to them, in which case it may be too late. Guinea pigs are able to differentiate between certain colors: try out the test on page 66.

try out the test on page 66.

Super Nose

Guinea pigs have an excellent sense of smell; they use their noses to learn new information: Where can I find food? Where are the other members of my group? Where are my enemies hiding? Strange odors, such as smoke, cooking smells, and cleaning products, smell very strong to a guinea pig.

Eavesdropping

Guinea pigs communicate with one another using a wide range of different noises. And a creature that has a lot to say also has a good ability to listen. With his highly sensitive hearing, he does not miss much—least of all the soft rustling of a bag of food. Be aware when watching TV or listening to music that a lot of noise makes guinea pigs feel uncomfortable or scared.

→ The Language of Scent

Guinea pigs also communicate with each other by using scent marks so that they can tell who is a family member and who is a stranger. A female attracts males with pheromones and also scent-marks her babies with her own urine.

Fussy Piggies

You will soon discover your guinea pig is a true gourmet with very particular likes and dislikes. Food that one guinea pig likes may be rejected by another in disgust. Some even pull faces at food they do not like! Unfortunately, they may also eat things they are not supposed to. If it tastes good, then they will eat it! So make sure you keep anything that is not good for them out of reach.

Sensitivity

Just as cats have whiskers, so do guinea pigs. They are found to the left and right of a guinea pig's nose. This allows them to feel out their surroundings in the dark. The whiskers are roughly the width of the body so that he can put his head in an entrance and figure out whether the rest of his body will fit through. Do not ever pluck or trim these hairs because he needs them!

Guinea pigs have super noses. The smell of cucumber has not gone unnoticed by this guinea pig!

Who is this? Scent messages play an important role for a guinea pig—he can learn a great deal about his companion just by sniffing him.

EXTRA
The Guinea Pig Translator

Guinea Pig Speak

→ Guinea pigs communicate differently with one another than they do with humans.

→ A guinea pig gives a loud whistle to draw attention to himself.

→ Guinea pigs communicate loudly and frequently among themselves and are able to recognize the individual call of another guinea pig.

→ Early in the morning, right after waking up, guinea pigs greet each other with a quiet vibrating gurgle.

→ Guinea pigs make excited squeaking noises when they find food.

→ If young animals are missing their parents, they give a loud, urgent squeak and then make whimpering sounds. The mother will rush to her baby's side and gurgle soothingly.

→ If he senses danger, the guinea pig "on duty" will emit a loud urgent whistle, and the group will quickly bolt to its hidey-hole. They change guards about every ten minutes so that each guinea pig gets a turn.

→ Any significant food finds are vocally reported to the others, and they respond with excited squeaking.

- → Guinea pigs make creaky, cooing, grunting sounds when trying to attract a mate.

- → Loud teeth sharpening, with the head lifted and the guinea pig strutting around, is a warning of a fight.

- → Pain and anxiety are expressed with a loud, anguished squeak or teeth chattering.

- → A chirp is a rarely heard sound that resembles a blackbird song and expresses frustration and stress. When making this noise, a guinea pig's whole body will shake.

- → If you pet a guinea pig, he may happily murmur, gurgle, and coo to himself.

- → As the group huddles close together in the evening, the guinea pigs coo softly.

- → Even during the night, you will sometimes hear a faint gurgling or chirruping noise.

- → The significance of every single one of their vast gurgling, cooing, grunting, whistling, and squeaking noises have not yet been studied in great detail.

Guinea Pigs and Other Pets

By now, you know that guinea pigs do not like living alone. They feel much more at ease when they have at least one companion or are part of a group. They also enjoy contact with human beings and can even form friendships with other animals.

Who is this? The scent says it all.

Guinea pigs and rabbits can sometimes become good friends and enjoy playing together, but they should not live in the same cage.

Birds of a Feather Flock Together

Naturally, guinea pigs prefer the company of their own species. But what happens if you want to introduce your guinea pig to one of your other pets? Because guinea pigs communicate best by using scents, it is a good idea to mingle the scents of the two different animals. Stroke your rabbit, for example, and then stroke your guinea pig. It is best that they get to know each other in a neutral space with room to run around. If there is a conflict, then make sure your guinea pig has an escape route—do not put the two animals in a small cage together. Read more about this on page 15.

Small Mammals

When introducing your rabbits to your guinea pigs, let them run around together and investigate one another slowly. Rabbits and guinea pigs tend to get along well, but they should still be kept in separate cages. One reason why they need their own cages is because these two animals have different dietary needs. For example, rabbits can synthesize their own vitamin C, but guinea pigs cannot and need it in their food. Rabbits and guinea pigs should be fed separately to make sure each animal is eating its appropriate food.

Dog, Cat, Guinea Pig
Guinea Pigs and Other Animals
Completely different species of animals can sometimes become fast friends. Even before meeting each other for the first time, they will already have smelled each other's scents. Your hand can act as a kind of scent messenger. Stroke your guinea pig and then get your dog or cat to sniff your hand. If you then stroke your dog or cat, then he will have the scent of the guinea pig on his fur.

First Meeting
Now it is time to take the next step and get the two animals together. Initially, keep your guinea pig in her cage and supervise your dog or cat as he carefully sniffs the cage. After the curiosity of both animals has been satisfied, praise and reward them both. This will create a positive experience, and once both animals are completely relaxed, you can supervise direct contact between the two. In some cases, nothing you do will ever make your animals become friends. It depends on their personalities. If your pets just do not get along, keep them away from each other so your guinea pig is not stressed.

→ Playing Together Under Supervision
No matter how well your guinea pig and dog or cat get along, never leave these animals alone together. Guinea pigs are prey animals for dogs and cats, and the hunting instinct could suddenly take over—then the friendship may be forgotten, and the guinea pig could be chased or even bitten.

Picking Up Your Piggy
Guinea pigs enjoy human contact, so it is important that you learn the correct way to handle your pet. First, stroke the guinea pig to prepare her for a cuddle. Then, place your hand gently under her chest but do not grip too tightly! Lift her off the ground and place your other hand under her bottom so she is sitting in both hands. Now you can lift her up and cradle her in your forearm. Support her with your other hand to make sure she does not fall. Do not let her jump out of your arms. Because guinea pigs do not have depth perception, they have no idea how high off the ground they are. Never pick your guinea pig up by her front legs or scruff of the neck because this will hurt her. Remember to teach every member of your family, especially your younger brothers or sisters, the correct way to pick up the guinea pig.

To pick up a guinea pig correctly, have one hand under the bottom and the other hand gently supporting his body.

Racing Around the House

Your guinea pig loves discovering new things on his daily run around the house.

Provide plenty of variety. Use boxes for caves and tubes for tunnels as well as a few hidden goodies to get even the laziest guinea pigs interested.

Guinea pigs need exercise! Their wild relatives spend much of the day guarding their habitats or roaming around looking for food. Your guinea pig is not really much different and has the natural urge to keep on the move.

Exercise Is the Best Health Care

Once your guinea pig is accustomed to his new home and has become tame with you, you can let him run about

in your house. Guinea pigs love to run around and satisfy their curiosity every day. Without a stimulating environment, they will become lethargic, obese, and prone to diseases. They should be let out of their cage for at least two to three hours a day, whether in the house or in an enclosure in the yard.

Housebreaking

With a little patience, guinea pigs can be housebroken. Guinea pigs naturally pick a corner of their cage to use as a bathroom. When let loose around the house, some will even return to their cages when they need to go to the bathroom without any encouragement from you.

Guinea Pig Toilet

While he is out of his cage, you could also provide your pet with a small litter box to use (see picture). Put a little bit of soiled bedding into the litter box, and then he will know what it is for. Remember to always use bedding; never use cat litter.

Safety in Numbers   Tip

It is a great idea to let your guinea pigs explore together and then return to their cage when they have had enough.

Water, Hay, and Hideaway

Tip

Make sure your guinea pig has access to water and hay while running around. He will also need somewhere to escape to if he wants a rest, so keep his hideaway nearby.

Clean Up Any Mishaps

Your guinea pig is bound to have small accidents every now and again. Do not yell at him—you will only end up scaring him. The fecal pellets can be easily swept up, and any puddles of urine can be cleaned up using a cloth and some hot, soapy water.

You can make a guinea pig obstacle course from cardboard boxes!

If you happen to notice that he appears to be looking for a place to go to the bathroom, pick him up and put him in his litter box. If he goes to the bathroom there, praise him and give him a treat. Guinea pigs are clean animals, and your guinea pig will quickly understand what you want him to do. Be sure to keep your guinea pig's litter box close to where he is. Guinea pigs have very small bladders and must urinate quite frequently.

How to Guinea Pig-Proof Your House

Before your guinea pig can go exploring, make your home—or at least one room—guinea pig-proof.

→ Electrical cords should be kept out of reach so that the guinea pig cannot gnaw on them.

→ Do not allow him to nibble at wallpaper, paint, varnish, or baseboards.

→ Close cabinet doors and drawers, and block any narrow cracks and crevices.

→ Put toxic substances, such as cleaning agents and medicines, out of reach.

→ Clear toys away.

→ Many houseplants are poisonous. Do not let your animals chew on them!

→ Open doors carefully—the guinea pig may be behind one of them!

→ Consider putting his outside playpen indoors to limit the space he can run around in and keep him safe.

→ Cover slippery floors or very shaggy carpets (your guinea pig may get his claws caught in them) with straw mats or patchwork rugs made of cotton.

→ For housebroken guinea pigs, provide a small litter box.

→ And finally, never allow your guinea pig to run around without supervision!

An Adventure Playground for Guinea Pigs

Running around the house is great fun, but pretty soon, your guinea pigs will get to know every nook and cranny—this is when it is time to add a bit more variety. Using simple equipment and a bit of imagination, you can design your own adventure playground for your guinea pigs, which will encourage them to discover something new each time.

Cavers

As animals that live in burrows and tunnels in the wild, guinea pigs love to investigate dark holes and little hideaways. You can create hideaways and tunnels using boxes, tubes, containers, and whatever else you can find so that your guinea pig can go on a miniature caving expedition.

A little caver on a discovery tour.

Fun for Indoors and Outdoors — Tip

Anything you create in the house for your adventure playground can also be taken outside in the yard. Do not forget to bring in any materials that may get wet outside, such as cardboard boxes and tubes.

Little Climbers

Guinea pigs will crawl and climb onto anything around them, and they are actually rather good at it. You could try using bricks to build a stairwell or make a ramp up to his hideaway using a piece of wood. One great thing about all this climbing is that it will help wear down his claws far more than the soft bedding in his cage.

Jungle Expedition

Grab a bunch of leafy branches—make sure they have not been treated with any fertilizers—from fruit trees, beech, hazel, and other safe plants and layer them around the room to create a jungle effect.

Your guinea pig can chew the leaves, bark, and buds and scurry in and out of the branches, climb over the top, and hide underneath, and he will also feel safe under the protective umbrella of the branches and leaves.

Well Fed and Fit

Guinea pigs like to have something to nibble while they are out and about. So not only is the adventure playground a great place to exercise, you can also make it a kind of food paradise as well. Hide little bits of food among the obstacles or fill a basket with hay and hide some vegetable pieces inside. Tie up a bunch of parsley and hang it just within reach of your guinea pig so that he has to stretch up to eat it. Carrots stuck into the bars of his cage are also a great idea. You could hide treats underneath a small upturned box or an empty toilet tissue tube full of hay. Then he will have to search out the treat in the hay.

Beach Party

You need a shallow container—for example, a box or a large flowerpot—and some fine, dry sand. The best type to use is sand for chinchillas, which you can buy from most pet supply stores. Sand from a sandpit is not suitable and may be dirty. Fill up the pot with sand and place it in front of your guinea pig so he can sniff it, climb into it, or even take a relaxing sand bath in it. This could get quite messy, so it is probably best to do it outside in his enclosure in the yard.

Climbing activities with snack breaks are great fun for guinea pigs.

FUN TIPS

Guinea Pig Circus

Cute and Talented

Show all your friends how clever your guinea pig is! Train her with these tricks, and your guinea pig will soon be the star of her very own circus!

Tightrope Walker

You need two bricks or two logs and a six-inch-long bridge. Now lure your guinea pig across the bridge with a treat. Soon she will be doing it all by herself.

Hurdler

Encourage your guinea pig over an obstacle with a treat. Give her a command, such as "Let's go!" and watch her climb over all sorts of obstacles!

Lion's Leap

Make yourself a small hoop and encourage your guinea pig to climb through it. Start off with the hoop on the ground and then gradually hold it up a bit higher. How high can your guinea pig go?

Farewell Bow

Guinea pigs rarely stand on their hind legs. Using a piece of your pet's favorite food, hold it above her nose and encourage her to stand up for it. You could support her on your leg while she does this, and this could be the finishing act in your circus display.

Rules for Guinea Pig Tamers

When you are having fun with your guinea pig circus, please follow these rules:

→ Do not make your guinea pig do something she does not want to do.

→ Reward her for every success with gentle pats and a small treat.

→ Do not practice for too long or your pet will lose interest.

→ Practice regularly, however, so that your guinea pig does not forget the tricks you have taught her.

Training Your Guinea Pig

So your guinea pig has a fantastically varied diet, a large cage with plenty of room to run around, and now even has an adventure playground to really let off some steam. Her physical needs are being met, but how about her intellectual needs? You can find out how smart she is and what she is capable of learning.

Guinea pigs can differentiate between certain colors, and this one has quickly learned that it is the yellow bowl that contains the food.

Through the Maze

Try building a maze out of cardboard boxes for your guinea pig. It does not have to be complicated, but it does need at least one dead end. Now put pieces of food in each section, leaving your guinea pig to find the right way through the maze all by herself. If you own multiple guinea pigs, you could have a competition. Which guinea pig is the fastest? Which one is the slowest? Does your guinea pig get faster each time she goes through the maze?

Red, Blue, Yellow

You need three or four different colored bowls—for example, red, light blue, dark blue, and yellow. Cover each bowl with a piece of cardboard. Now put some food in the yellow bowl. Of course, at first, your guinea pig will find the food simply by sniffing it out, but as you do it again and again, you will notice that she runs straight to the yellow bowl with no hesitation, even if there is no food in there.

Pretty Smart

Now try this: give a whistle or ring a small bell, and when she comes to investigate, feed your guinea pig. Do this each and every time you feed her and as soon as she hears the whistle, she will come running!

Plenty of Time and Lots of New Ideas

The most important thing of all: you should spend as much time as possible cuddling and playing with your guinea pig. By taking care of her and paying her attention, she will be at her happiest and learn new things, whether it is discovering a new object in her cage or her adventure playground. Use the ideas in this book to help you keep your guinea pig's mind sharp and active.

A Match Made in Heaven? Test

How well do you know your guinea pigs? And how well do your guinea pigs know you?

- [ ] My guinea pigs begin to squeal as soon as they see me coming.

- [ ] When I have a tasty treat in my hand, my guinea pigs come running.

- [ ] I know what makes my guinea pigs the most curious.

- [ ] I know what makes my guinea pigs the most anxious.

- [ ] My guinea pigs love to be stroked and enjoy playing with their toys.

- [ ] My guinea pigs spend time running around.

- [ ] My guinea pigs explore new play and exercise equipment with curiosity and enthusiasm.

- [ ] When I rustle my hand in the hay, my guinea pigs come over to investigate.

- [ ] When I hide treats in the cage, my guinea pigs look for them straightaway.

Have you answered all of these questions with a "yes"?

Congratulations! You and your guinea pigs make a great team!

At a Glance

Understanding Your Guinea Pig

Suitable Material for Guinea Pig Games

For the cage, outdoor enclosure, and adventure playground, only use nontoxic materials that are safe for the guinea pig to chew on.

Suitable items include

→ guinea pig "furniture" from pet shops, made from untreated wood

→ tubes made from clay, cork, bark, or wood

→ woven straw mats

→ baskets made from untreated straw

→ plain cardboard (no print)

→ clean bricks

Guinea Pig Senses

Sight

Guinea pigs are a bit shortsighted but have an almost 360-degree view and can distinguish between colors.

Hearing

Guinea pigs have fantastic hearing, which is about the same as a cat or dog. You should avoid making loud or high frequency noises in their presence.

Smell

Guinea pigs have superb noses! In fact, most of their communication is through scent, and strong odors, such as cleaning products or cigarette smoke, smell very strong to guinea pigs.

Taste

Guinea pigs are true gourmets, and they have their own individual likes and dislikes.

Touch

With the sensitive whiskers on their heads, guinea pigs can find their way in the dark.

Exercise Is Great Fun

→ Guinea pigs need to satisfy their urge to move in order to stay healthy.

→ Let your guinea pig out of her cage for at least two to three hours a day.

→ Make sure she is safe—guinea-pig-proof your home before you let her out.

→ Always try something new: build and create new playground and gym equipment with tasty treats hidden inside.

→ Do not forget to provide her with hay, water, and a hideaway while she is playing.

Objects for Play

→ Tubes made of clay, cork, bark, or wood are ideal for her to hide in.

→ Use stairs or bricks so she can climb onto the roof of her hideaway.

→ Branches and twigs are great for sniffing and nibbling.

→ From time to time, all guinea pigs love a good sand bath.

→ Treats in high places make her stretch up and reach high.

→ Be a toy! Lie on the floor and let your guinea pig sniff you and climb over your legs and arms! Give her a cuddle!

Translated from the German edition by Claire Mullen.

Edited and produced by Enslow Publishers, Inc.

Originally published in German.

© 2007 Franckh-Kosmos Verlags-GmbH & Co. KG, Stuttgart, Germany
Angela Beck, *Meerschweinchen*

Library of Congress Cataloging-in-Publication Data

Beck, Angela.
   [Meerschweinchen. English]
   Guinea pigs : keeping and caring for your pet / Angela Beck.
      pages cm. — (Keeping and caring for your pet)
   Includes bibliographical references and index.
   Summary: "Discusses how to choose and care for a guinea pig,
      including diet, behaviors, housing, grooming, exercise, popular
      breeds, and vet care" —Provided by publisher.
   ISBN 978-0-7660-4184-4
   1. Guinea pigs as pets—Juvenile literature. I. Title.
   SF459.G9B428 2013
   636.935—dc23
                    2012038631

Paperback ISBN 978-1-4644-0299-9

Printed in the United States of America

052014 Lake Book Manufacturing, Inc., Melrose Park, IL

10 9 8 7 6 5 4 3 2

Photo Credits: Color photos taken by Ulrike Schanz especially for the purposes of this book except Juniors Bildarchiv, pp. 8 (top), 21, 27 (bottom); Shutterstock.com, p. 1.

Cover Photos: All from Shutterstock.com except author photo (back) by Ulrike Schanz. *Main photo:* orange and white guinea pig. *Bottom, from left to right:* gray guinea pig, brown and orange guinea pig, white and black guinea pig, black and white Peruvian guinea pig. *Back:* orange, white, and brown long-haired guinea pig.

Index

Further Reading

Books

Alderton, David. *Looking After Small Pets.* Wigston, Leicester, England: Southwater, 2012.

Birmelin, Immanuel. *Guinea Pigs.* Hauppauge, N.Y.: Barron's Educational Series, 2008.

Mahoney, Myra. *Mini Encyclopedia of Guinea Pigs: Breeds and Care.* Dorking, Surrey, England: Interpet Publishing, 2010.

Internet Addresses

ASPCA: Guinea Pig Care
http://www.aspca.org/pet-care/small-pet-care/guinea-pig-care.aspx

The Humane Society of the United States: Guinea Pigs
http://www.humanesociety.org/animals/guinea_pigs/

American Cavy Breeders Association
http://www.acbaonline.com/